Soul of a Broken Woman

KAREN BROWN

ROMELO Publications

Soul of a Broken Woman
Copyright ©2020 by Karen Brown

This title is also available as an eBook. ISBN: 978-1-9990430-7-0

Requests for information should be addressed to:

Romelo Publications
406-134 Queen Street East
Brampton, ON. Canada
L6V 1B2
www.romelopublications.com

This print edition: ISBN: 978-1-9990430-6-3

Non-Fiction

Romelo Publications 2020

Library and Archives Canada:

Brown, Karen.
        Soul of a Broken Woman
ISBN: 978-1-9990430-6-3
1.   Memoir
2.   Christian Life
3.   Self-Help

Any information, data, and references are offered as a resource. They are not intended in any way to be or imply an endorsement by Romelo Publications.

All rights reserved. No part of this publication may be reproduced, stored in a retrieval system, or transmitted in any form or by any means - electronic, mechanical, photocopy, recording, or any other - except for brief quotations in printed reviews, without the prior permission of the publisher.

Cover design: Romelo Publications
Interior design: Cre8tive Design

Printed in Canada

Table of Content

Introduction

Acknowledgment

Foreword

Chapter 1: The Story of My Life

Chapter 2: Wounds of a Woman

Chapter 3: Let God Heal Your Wounds

Chapter 4: Your Life is not a Secret to God

Chapter 5: Breaking Free from The Pain of your Past

Chapter 6: Greatness Lies within you

Chapter 7: Never Quit on Yourself (Be that confident woman)

Chapter 8: Overcoming

Chapter 9: Life's Lesson

Biblical Scriptures and Quotations

Reflections & Questions

Introduction

My name is Karen Brown, a severely mentally, physically, and emotionally abused survivor. I struggled with low self-esteem, bitterness, anger, and hatred for people who hurt me. I was severely abused as a child and this abuse continued into my adult life. However, I was able to overcome all these struggles and obstacles. I am now thriving and living a fulfilling, God-fearing, and successful life.

In this life we all have struggles; we experience much pain at times. These pains and struggles sometimes come about by the people we trust: our family, friends, and those closest to us. You can overcome hurt and suffering, but you will have to go through a process that does not happen overnight. You will need to go through self-acknowledgement, counseling, and much prayer. "Trust in the Lord with all thine heart; and lean not unto thine own understanding. In all thy ways acknowledge him, and he shall direct thy path." (Proverbs 3:5-6 - KJV).

For all the pain and suffering that I have experienced, I believe my purpose is to help women, especially those who are single and hurting, overcome the many adversities they face in their lives. I hope that my story will give courage and hope to those women who feel helpless and dismayed.

Acknowledgment

Writing a book about the story of my life is an incredible process. I had sleepless nights and spent countless hours in making sure my memoir was captured in its entirety. I want to thank God for making this possible for me because without Him, I would not write this book.

To my family: my mother and step-father; I cannot imagine life without them. My children are a source of strength; everything I do, I do for them; they are my lifeline. They sustained me in ways that I never knew I needed.

Thanks to Romelo Publications for the opportunity to publish my book.

I am immensely grateful to the Transforming Dreams Mentorship Program, and being mentored by Victoria A. Morgan, who have allowed me to use the program as my personal learning laboratory in completing my book. She was able to help me in taking my vision into manifestation.

I want to acknowledge and thank Palmonia Gordon, who made a huge contribution through her Order It Mentorship Program in helping me to realize and bring my blueprint to reality.

Thank you so much to Mr. Lloyd Morrison at Lloyd Morrison Photography, who did an amazing job demonstrating his photographic skills. You took some truly amazing pictures which I will treasure for a lifetime.

Thanks to Zackariah, an amazing and talented Book Cover Designer. The book cover design really captured the essence of my story; it is beautiful.

Finally, to all who have been a part of my journey, I am forever grateful.

Foreword

Black woman, you are a treasure to this world. It is such a shame that others choose to deny your light, intentionally degrading and withholding the love, joy and peace you ever so deserve. Instead, you must fight for the basic right to be as you are. It's time to change the narrative."

- Christen Palmer

Examining the definition of survivor, we think of someone who has overcome or continues to live despite adverse challenges and experience. I firmly believe that to survive is an act of heroism when life has dealt its worst.

We hear of heroes in fictional narratives as representations of what it is to survive, yet we neglect to consider that there are those we know and have come to love who are dealing with personal traumas that most could not withstand; those whose lives behind closed doors are a living torment.

Despite all that Karen has endured, she has not just survived, but can now be a blessing and source of encouragement and motivation to other black women. As a long-standing friend, Karen has persevered when obstacles presented told her she could not go any further. When backed into a corner, she stood her ground. With the support of friends, family and her relationship to the Most-High, Karen could stand on her own two feet.

I am proud to see her growth. As with the Lotus flow, traversing through the muddy waters of life, she finds her way to reach the sunlight that transforms her into the beautiful flower she is.

Jacqueline Palmer, A Dear Friend

WHAT PEOPLE ARE SAYING ABOUT THIS BOOK:

It has been a pleasure to meet with Karen Brown. It started with one courageous conversation in counselling therapy four years ago. Karen is a woman who had been abused in both family and two marriage relationships. Karen Brown has created a blueprint for facing this specter of the treatment that could await many other women. Through her thoughtful balance between content and message is her story and humor of the Soul of a Broken Woman.

This book will give women the courage and tools to deal with and overcome brokenness and crisis because they are able to make wise decisions to deal with the Soul of a Broken Woman. Women will be empowered to have honest, momentous conversations with women they love, cherish, and what is important in their lives. This book will diminish the fear of the unknown and replace it with hope, joy, respect, understanding, and peace of mind. Isn't that the best way to learn? Just think about your own daughters, granddaughters, sisters, and nieces who have been wounded, broken, and dismayed because no one ever expressed to them the Soul of a Broken Women.

> ***Dr. Rev. Patricia Keith, Ph.D. Counselor,***
> ***Therapist at Break Free Family Centre.***
> ***breakfreecounsel@rogers.com***

When I was first introduced to Karen Brown, what struck me was the smile in her voice. You know those people who, while they are telling you the sky is falling and you look up and see that it is actually 'falling,' then you look at them and see they are smiling, that is Karen. Karen and I connected almost immediately, maybe it was her honesty in letting me know, "I have followed you and watched you for a long time on social media, but I never say anything." An observer, yes, but so much more. A woman of action who did not hesitate to sign up and step on campus so she could learn the secret of how to 'Order it;' order whatever she wanted in life. So, when I got the call about writing the foreword for "Soul of a Broken Woman," I smiled, no I grinned. I was elated. Karen is fulfilling her dream.

I remembered the day when I picked up my bag to go to work and the thought of going postal made sense, but almost instantly, I knew it was the end of that road for me. I had completed about twenty-five years at the post office, and I struggled every day to get up and keep going. A divorcee, by choice, with five children; what could I do? What did I know except what seemed like pain, frustration, and failure? So, my journey began; it was a decision to walk away from the post office and follow a path to write books, travel, and tell stories to help women step into their greatness. It was that journey that led me to Karen.

Do you know how many women are living life stuck? They wake up looking, longingly, waiting for someone to come along and show them the way out of their mess;

someone to help. Karen has always had a passion for helping women but not just any woman: single women who are struggling and looking for more. When she stepped on campus to do a course with me, I smiled when I listened to her, even as I wondered: how is it possible for someone who has experienced so much pain to radiate so much energy, have so much faith and is always smiling. Soul of a Broken Woman is a fitting title for Karen's story because it delves into the depth and core of who she is as a human being. You will cry, pause to catch your breath, then applaud as you realize her spirit may have been shattered, shaken but her soul, hmmm, that part way down deep inside, that is something else and the essence of her story.

When Karen told me of her dreams and her desire to publish this book, to have a group for women: Single-Mothers-Can-be-Successful-Despite-Many-Objections, I believed her. I believed she would do it. Now it is here! With her spirit of resilience, determination, and made-up-my-mind-to-succeed, I had no doubt she would do it. Her passion to help women runs so deep that she has embarked on a lifelong dream of becoming a family lawyer; a decision born from an understanding that the pain women endure can be lessened if they have someone who truly understands to guide them.

Why should you read the Soul of a Broken Woman? Simply because it is your soul. It will offer you an anchor, a chain, a place to rest and gather your strength, gather your thoughts, remind yourself of who you are and of what is possible for you. It is about knowing that others believe in you; understanding that it is doable. Yes, it is hard but you can. Why? Because Karen is willing to open up and be vulnerable to let you know how, to show you the way so you too can stand on the mountaintop and say, "Yes! I may have the soul of a broken woman but I can sing, I can win, I can survive and will survive."

"What inspired you to write this book?" I asked. The reply was short, sweet, and to the point: "Things have to change!" Pausing for a brief moment, Karen said oh so softly, almost like she was still thinking, "I have to break the silence!" Ironically, her answer reminded me of the story a mentor shared with me many years ago when I was studying to be a Christian Counselor: "A couple and their three-year-old son sat at the dinner table eating in silence. The couple had had a fight and there was tension in the air. They were not speaking to each other. Suddenly, unable to take the tension any more, the little boy yelled, 'Can you please stop the shouting?'"

Yes, it is time to break the silence. It is time to let you know that in spite of the hardships, the trials and obstacles you have faced in life, there is still hope. Karen's story is designed to help you on your journey. I believe it will also remind you that one day you will help someone on their journey. So, hurry now, start reading, we don't have much time to lose.

Palmonia Gordon
CEO - ORDER IT

Chapter One
THE STORY OF MY LIFE

I was born in Jamaica, but my mother migrated to Canada to make a better life for us in the late seventies. I do not know my father, so I lived with my grandmother from a very tender age. Life with my grandmother was great until other grand-children came to live with us. It was sometimes difficult, but my grandmother always took good care of us; God bless her soul.

At about six or seven years old, I went to live with my grandfather's family in the same district. Living with us were my two aunts, grandfather, his wife, and my cousin. Sometimes my aunt's children, who were not permanently living with us, visited. I started staying with them on a short-term basis because a family member had a broken hip and needed someone to stay with her. So, I stayed while they went to evening church services or any other engagement that required their presence. As time went by, it became a permanent living arrangement.

These persons were my family, so I thought living with them was good, and life would be a little more comfortable as they were considered middle class. My grandmother was less fortunate than they were, but little did I know that my life was about to become a nightmare. I was treated worse than Cinderella, not because they could not do better, but because they were cruel people; they treated me badly.

My aunts (my mother's sisters) treated me very badly. I was treated like a slave or, in other words, I was treated like a real-life Cinderella. Every morning before school, I had to clean the house, tend to the goats, cut grass for the young kids, feed the pigs and chickens, and sweep the yard. This was difficult because, by the time I got to school, I would be very tired.

Soul of a Broken Woman

I had a very rough childhood. My uncle-in-law, the husband to one of my aunts, attempted to rape me once, but I escaped. There was a lot of emotional, mental, and physical abuse at times that was unbearable. Believe it or not, it was a Christian home. I felt like dying sometimes, but I always believed that my mother would come and get me one day so I held on. I was not allowed to call my mother on the phone, nor did I have her number; it was never given to me. When my mother sent money for me, my aunt took a great portion of it and told me the currency fell. Of course, I had no knowledge of the currency, so I took whatever I got.

My mother would send clothes for me, and my aunts would share them with their children before I got any. My mother did not know any of this because I could not tell her; if I did, my aunt would beat me as she always does. I did not have free access to my own mother except for times when I would write to her, and even then, I could not tell her of my pain. I feared that if I told my mother what I was going through and my aunts found out, they would beat me.

One day, my aunt tossed a stone at me for not doing something she asked me to do. I was running, and the stone hit me in the back of the head, and I fell to the ground. My cousin had to throw water on me so I could regain consciousness. The scar is on my head to this day; it is one I will never forget. There were times when my aunts' children would sit around the table that I set, and eat with a knife and fork, while I would sometimes sit on the back steps of the veranda, eating from a plastic plate and drinking from a plastic cup.

My life was rough, but I believed my mother would come and get me one day. By the time I was about ten years old, my mother came for a visit. I did not bother to tell her anything because I feared that I would be punished when she returned to Canada. My mother filed for me to migrate to Canada to be with her; I was very excited.

One Saturday in 1985, I was scheduled for a 3:00

p.m. flight to Canada to be with my mother. My aunt woke me up at 5:00 a.m. I only had enough time to say goodbye to my dear grandmother. She took me to the Montego Bay Airport and left me in the care of the checking agents. The checking agents escorted me to the pilot's and flight attendant's waiting area, who then escorted me to the plane for my departure from Jamaica. When it was time for me to board the plane, I did not have anyone to wave goodbye to; I was left all alone as if I were an alien on some deserted island.

I arrived in Canada to be with my mother that night. It was heaven on earth; I was very happy that I was taken away from the horrible pit I was living in. Life for me was blooming in every possible way. I had good relationships with my mother and step-father; I attended and graduated from high school, I graduated from college, and I had given my life to the Lord.

There was only one thing that was left to complete this wonderful life and that was marriage. In 1985, just about the same time I arrived in Canada, I met a guy from Grenada about the same age as me. We became friends, not knowing he would one day become my husband. We attended the same church. Our friendship would later develop into a wonderful love affair in June 1990. We loved each other, we both loved the Lord, and we were always active in the church.

We got married in 1996, and life was great until my first child was born in 1997. My husband started to think things looked greener on the other side and decided to have an affair. The mental, emotional, and verbal abuse began all over again. My self-esteem started to deteriorate; the feeling of rejection and self-pity began to take hold of me. I kept it all to myself, fearing the unknown and always wondering if I would be able to manage on my own if he left. I was also worried about the embarrassment of being divorced and what people would say.

We had three children by this time, and it was unbearable, but I still refused to let anyone know my ordeal. Thank God I had a very good friend who I trusted. She was always encouraging me to be strong and trust God;

she was the only person I felt I could talk to, so I confided in her. Even though I talked to her, I still did not release everything to her because I was afraid of the embarrassment I had always been experiencing. The situation got so bad that I attempted suicide. I tried to take pills, run my car off the road, and jump off a bridge, but none of these worked because there was always someone who intervened or interrupted what I was about to do. I knew then that suicide was never the answer to my problems.

I sought help through the church but the pastor took advantage of my vulnerability and caused discomfort for me though-out the church. I felt like life no longer had any meaning for me; I felt I had no self-worth. Jesus kept me through it all, and He would not let me go, even though many times I wanted to let go. Jesus reminded me that He would never leave me or forsake me.

I again confided in my friend, who invited me to a celebrate recovery program. I was a bit reluctant because I did not care about my life anymore or thought anything or anyone could help me. I showed up to the program and met with some of the most wonderful people on the planet. Although I did not feel like being in the program at times, it was as though I was brought there weekly by some supernatural force. The program helped me unlock the hurt and past hang-ups in my life, although I still felt as if the host of hell had doubled in my life.

The changes God had made in my life through celebrating recovery were patience, courage, boldness and forgiveness. There is still work that needs to be done in these areas, but I have learned to trust people, be open, and be close with God.

To those who are reading my story and maybe going through difficult times, I encourage you to try the recovery program. Everything may not change all at once, but do not forget, everything did not get to where it was all at once. Trust God. Proverb 3:5-6 says, "Trust in the Lord with all thine heart; and lean not unto thine own understanding. In all thy ways acknowledge him, and he shall direct thy paths." (KJV).

Soul of a Broken Woman

The celebrating recovery program is a balanced biblical program that helps individuals to overcome their many hurts and hang-ups that life brought them. This program was launched by the pastor for Saddleback Church, Rick Warren. After going through this program, my life was grand again. I got divorced and started over as a single mother with three beautiful children. Caring for my children was a challenge, but I am motivated, committed, and determined to live a fulfilling life with my head held high. Single mothers can make it despite much opposition; we do not have to be afraid, and we do not have to be ashamed, especially if you became a single mother by no fault of yours. I went back to school to upgrade my skills, settled into an amazing job, purchased my first home, and acquired a few positions in my life. My children and I were doing well, and I felt like I was whole again. My relationship with God was going great; I was alright.

In the year 2009, life was blissful, and I felt it was time to move on to the next era of my life. I found love, but not just any love; my childhood sweetheart found his way back into my life after many years of us being apart. We grew up together in a little district called Calabar in Trelawny, Jamaica. We attended the same school and church, and we often played together. We knew each other from childhood, and we both knew that one day we would become soul mates. My parents did not want me to marry anyone from our community. My mother always wanted me to find someone in the city, someone who may offer more opportunities since we were from a poor family and community. Despite this opposition and barrier, our love prevailed. In 1985, I migrated to Canada to live with my mother. Though I could not make much contact with the love of my life, we never ceased to inquire about each other because the love was still there.

I visited Jamaica in 1990 to attend my grandmother's funeral. We encountered the same barrier where there was little hope of us ever being together, especially when we had no direct contact with each other. So, the love of my life married another girl, and they had three children. I also got married with three children. My marriage dissolved, and I was separated in 2003 and finally divorced in 2007. On July 31, 2009, after nineteen years of not returning to Jamaica, I decided to visit so I could get away from the hurt for a while. I thought of him but felt there was no hope since he was already married with children, not knowing that his marriage was also dissolved.

No one was expecting my visit to Jamaica; it was a surprise. I spent ten days in Jamaica: two days in our district and eight days at a resort trying to find peace. On day two of my visit to the district, we met for a very short while, and we exchanged numbers. That was the only encounter we had while I was in Jamaica. I was not aware of any problems, and I did not want to interfere with his marriage.

I returned to Canada in August of 2009 after my short vacation. I thought I had lost his number because I could not find it anywhere. I was really disappointed in my carelessness of not securing the number properly until one day when I was organizing my handbag, there was the piece of paper with his number. I was so excited; I felt like I was alive again. The very thought of him gave my life a new meaning. I contacted him, and he was as excited to hear from me as I was excited to hear from him. It was at this time that I learned his marriage was also dissolved. It was an emotional moment for both of us. We were both grown adults, and now we were able to make decisions for ourselves. We were finally free to decide our destiny and to choose who we both wanted to be with.

As the months turned into years, we grew closer to each other. Our main source of communication was phone and Skype. We talked to each other, almost daily. Although I could not visit Jamaica as often as I would like to, seeing him on Skype and hearing his voice was always a moment I looked forward to. We often talked about getting married and growing old together. We grew up in the church; he was a pastor and I was a

Christian. We always believed that our faith in God and His will for our lives would bring us together. As such, we decided that I would visit Jamaica in 2012 so we could get married.

In late November 2011, he was introduced to an opportunity to work on the Farm Work Program in Canada. He arrived in Canada in early January of 2012. We frequently communicated through telephone and, sometimes, through weekend visits since he had to work and he lived four hours away. I often drove up to visit him, or he would take the Greyhound Bus to Toronto or a chartered taxi to London, Ontario, where his cousin and I would pick him up. Our love for each other grew stronger and stronger each moment we were together. We thank God that He brought us together.

After several months of intense courtship, he proposed, and I said yes. We got married in September 2012. It was a moment that neither of us will ever forget; a moment in time that is wrapped in love so tightly, it will never fade away. Our love for each other is a priceless treasure.

The moment we made our vows, I felt the ache in my heart for the countless tears of past years when we were kept apart, and now the one moment I have waited for so long had come. We both know that our days would be filled with unconditional love and laughter as we journey through our destiny and, of course, having God at the center of it all. Our children, love, and the bond that grew between us would always keep us together.

Although my husband and I could not spend every moment with each other because he had to honor his work contract, our love and our strong faith in God kept us. "And we know that in all things God works for the good of those who love him, who[a] have been called according to his purpose." (Romans 8:28 - NIV). We had hope that our destiny and faith would bring us together in one place. We used the Via Rail from Windsor to Brampton as our means of transportation due to weather conditions.

In 2013, we were finally united, and now our lives truly began. We were living together for the first time as man and wife. Things were great; he got a job, he now had his permanent residence status, and everything was looking so bright. We decided to sponsor his children to join us in Canada so that we would have this happy blended family.

About a year into the marriage, I noticed little changes in my husband. He was not as caring or committed as he was earlier in the marriage. He would not contribute to the household as a husband should; he would leave for hours without saying where he was and communication between us was difficult. The strain of taking on the household's full responsibility was starting to take a toll on me, but just like before, I kept it to myself, fearing the embarrassment of what people would say. Here I was, again thanking and asking God for His grace and mercy towards my children and me. It was the Lord who kept me through my past ordeal, and I knew He would never leave me.

I started to journal my life: "Tonight is one of those nights, Lord, when I really miss my husband. I really don't know if he feels the same, but You know all things." I was starting to feel like a "married, single mother." When I look back over the entire situation, the Lord knows I only had good intentions for us, but maybe I was asking for too much, or maybe I was living in a fantasy with a man who was only interested in his own selfish gain. In any case, it is over and, in the past, so now I had to look ahead and be positive.

It was now time for my husband's children to arrive in Canada since their sponsorship was approved. We needed to find a bigger space, but my husband would not cooperate with me. Instead, he was comparing our culture to other cultures; individuals who lived in crowded spaces. I did not want that for us, especially not for his children. I wanted us to live comfortably. Although he would not cooperate and join with me in acquiring a bigger space, I went ahead and ensured that adequate living space was prepared and ready for his children on their arrival to Canada.

I started to feel stressed, confused and overwhelmed

with his behaviour. I did not know or even suspected that his intentions were to bring his children to Canada and move into his own apartment. To my surprise, he did just that simply because he refused to contribute to the household expenses that came with acquiring a larger space. However, he was able to pay rent instead of taking care of his own responsibilities. I was very disappointed and hurt because I already acquired a larger space for everyone. This was our first separation.

Situations and living conditions got difficult for my husband and his children so I decided to accept them back into my home. Things were going well for a little while, but then he started to change again. I started to feel a sense of emotional and psychological trauma. Again, the responsibility for the home rested solely on me, and again, it started to become unbearable. So I asked them to leave once more; this was the third time. He waited until I left for work to get a moving truck and moved out his belongings without my knowledge of his whereabouts.

Life got to him again, so he returned another time, and of course, I took him back. It was then that I realized that in pleasing others, I ended up hurting myself. I am the one who was always taking care of the family; everyone was always dependent on me. My greatest weakness was not being able to say no. My husband had no sense of responsibility as a husband and father; everything rested on me. I always had to be the one planning for tomorrow and taking care of each day.

I found myself facing chronic emotional abuse once again. I was falling into depression and anxiety. I was often by myself, even with my husband at home. Our communication deteriorated drastically, intimacy was almost non-existent, and self-doubt started to damage my confidence. My husband had the tendency to think that everything and everyone else was more important than me. He spoke highly of me to others in public, but at home, it was not so.

I refused to tell anyone about my home life, especially my family, because I was afraid they would say, "I told you so." My husband's despicable behavior was shameful, and I thought to myself, "Do I have to put up with this or do I stay and take it?" I stayed with him and provided for myself. He worked, but his jobs would not last for any extended time because he always found something to complain about until he eventually left the job. The small contribution he gave towards the family was not enough.

I felt so emotionally drained, and I found myself sometimes excusing my husband's poor behavior and lack of responsibility. He was quite secretive; he would go out and not tell me his whereabouts. Therefore, I was never entirely sure what he was doing and when he was doing it. I was never really relaxed but I told myself that life was beautiful and I could make something beautiful out of it. Even with feeling emotionally distressed, I learned to embrace myself despite the adversities and challenges I faced. I often cried but I reminded myself that these experiences and challenges I was facing would not last forever; they were here to make me stronger and wiser.

I had to hold on and not give up even when I felt like it.

My husband and I separated for the last time. He refused to stand up and take the responsible role of being a husband, father, and leader in our marriage. I, therefore, refused to continue being emotionally and mentally victimized in an unstable marriage. I had to value myself enough to set boundaries for my life, and if loving him was hurting me, then I had to step back and evaluate myself. My husband always thought of himself and his plans. His family always seemed to take precedence over our family and me.

I wore a beautiful smile on the outside, but the girl on the inside was something to imagine. Throughout my life, I never experience so much hurt and pain. So many scars was in heart that I sometimes wondered where my strength came from. However, I was reminded that my strength came from God, my sustainer. When someone looked at me, I would say to myself: if only that person knew the pain that was within my heart and how much I was screaming for help from within. I held it together. I did not know how I found the strength within me to do it, but I held on to hope.

Most times, when I was alone, at bedtime or when no one was looking, I would cry endless tears. I know I gave my best in everything I did. It was either my best or nothing at all.

Life treated me so badly since I was a child; I experienced pain and heartaches. Everything for me has always been a fight, but I know I am not a quitter. I will not quit on life; I will not allow my life to end before my purpose is fulfilled. So when I fall down, I will always get back up stronger because I am a fighter, I am a warrior, and I am a winner. I never quit; I will not quit. I have a purpose in life, and I will fulfill that purpose.

Life is so unfair. I do not believe I deserve to face all these obstacles and challenges throughout my life, but who am I not to go through them? Remember, Jesus Christ came down from heaven and bore a cross that He did not deserve.

In late 2019, my challenges became overwhelming. I went through heart surgery; I suffered a heart attack after the surgery because of the amount of stressors in my life. I now have a broken heart and other health conditions, but I know who God is, and I know that I am healed by His stripes. Life's challenges affected my health, and I kept it to myself. Many people did not know, and many still do not know. I would go to work, feel sick, and have to be taken to the hospital. This happened on more than one occasion. I kept it all to myself and suffered. Even though I went to church, I still would not tell anyone because I had experienced pain and suffering at the hand of church folks.

Everything around me was deteriorating, but I held on to hope. I held on to my faith in God, and I held on to assured victory. I chose not to give up because God promised me that He would never leave or forsake me, and He keeps His promises. I am here today because of God's grace and His mercy towards me. I would appear to be strong or a tough girl who helps everyone who came around her; I would give until I felt it in my soul. I gave everyone everything that I could. I only wished that someone would give the same to me. I tried my best to ensure that everyone around me got the best of me; sometimes, I gave out of nothing. My smiles would cover my brokenness; I smiled to hide my pain.

"He heals the brokenhearted and binds up their wounds." (Psalm 147:3 - NIV).

Our pain is not hidden from God; instead, He offers us relief and healing if we show Him our brokenness and invite Him into the pain.

Chapter 2
WOUNDS OF A WOMAN

There are wounds that lie within a woman that only God can heal. However, this can only happen if the wounded allow God to manifest His love, strength, and wisdom through her. God healed me, and to those women who are abused and battered, God wants to heal you as well.

In chapter one, you read my story. I was a severely wounded woman who survived much abuse and pain from childhood; a wounded married woman who went through two marriages and now a single mother who is thriving with my head held high. None of this would have been possible if it was not for the grace of God.

My experiences in life taught me to be humble. They

have also taught me how to appreciate myself and know my self-worth. All the pain and hurt that I experienced have enabled me to be used by God to help other hurting women. It is not easy for someone who has never been where I have been to counsel or advise another hurting woman. Unless you have walked in my shoes, you will never know what I feel. I believe that God wants me to use my life experiences to help other hurting women. Hebrews 4:15-16 (NIV), "For we do not have a high priest who is unable to empathize with our weaknesses, but we have one who has been tempted in every way, just as we are—yet he did not sin. Let us then approach God's throne of grace with confidence, so that we may receive mercy and find grace to help us in our time of need."

When I look back over my life, and see where God has brought me from and where I am today, I give God thanks. I have suffered at the hands of my aunts as a child, abused, made to think that I have no worth, treated like a real-life Cinderella, battered, beaten, and treated less than. I suffered much pain as a child. There was an attempted rape. My uncle-in-law attempted to rape me at ten years old. I was vulnerable, weak, and helpless, but God rescued me. God saw the good in me when no one else did. Today you may be going through some really tough times but do not give up hope; God sees you when no one else does, He sees the best in you, and He will rescue you; there is hope. God can take what Satan meant for evil and make it into something beautiful. He will take what is wrong and make it right.

Let me tell you, all the pain and suffering that I have been through; I was very angry, bitter, full of hatred, including self-hate, because I know I did not deserve to be treated the way I was treated. God has a way of making things right. He is an on-time God; there is a word, and a solution for every aspect of life, and God assures me in Isaiah 41-15-17 (NIV): "See, I will make you into a threshing sledge, new and sharp, with many teeth. You will thresh the mountains and crush them, and reduce the hills to chaff. You will winnow them, the wind will pick them up, and a gale will blow them away. But you will rejoice in the Lord and glory in the Holy One of Israel. The poor and needy search for water, but there is none; their tongues are parched with thirst. But I the Lord will answer them; I, the God of Israel, will not forsake them."

You may be shattered but not broken; wounded, but time will heal. Trust God, and He will work it out for your good. Let go and let God have His way. He will make things alright. Gospel singer, Tye Tribbett, explained this in his song entitled "He Turned It": "Yes, there were times in my life when I thought I would never make it. I almost went down; I was out for the count; I was through, but it was then when I thought it would end that I stood up again; what hell had for evil God turned it around for my good."

I went through much abuse and feelings of hurt and hopelessness. I cried out to God just like David did in Psalm 40:1-2 (NKJV): "I waited patiently for the Lord; and He inclined to me, and heard my cry. He also brought me up out of a horrible pit, out of the miry clay, and set my feet upon a rock, and established my steps."

Chapter 3
LET GOD HEAL YOUR WOUNDS

Sometimes we go through so many things and we think we are alone. God actually wants to use those wounds to heal us. We have to go through some things in life; however, God's purpose will prevail. We sometimes hide those wounds and scars so deep within that we consider them dead. One day our inner darkness and fear will become light. God will use the inner darkness to heal the broken heart. He wants to take our wounds and heal us.

We are soldiers in God's army, and He wants to build us. We sometimes may feel rejected, bruised, abused, and neglected, but one thing that is certain is: Jesus will never reject us. Jesus will never abuse us because

He loves us. God sent Jesus Christ into this world. He felt our pain, sees the scars that we have buried so deep within us, and He will heal us. So, we should take your burdens to the Lord and leave them there.

As I mentioned in chapter one, the brokenness, hurt, pain, bruises, those scars are so deep; they are buried within me, but there is hope. As I am writing this book, I pray that God will heal the broken bones, mend the broken pieces, and put the brokenness back together again.

In chapter one, I also spoke about my wounds; how my aunts treated me so badly. I cried because the wounds within me were so bad. There were emotional scars, mental scars, and physical scars on my body, which hurt really bad. I was so badly wounded, I felt all alone, rejected, and as if there was no hope for me, but God was right there. He never gave up on me. God sees what man cannot see. Unlike man, who looks at the outward appearance, God looks at the heart; He saw my pain. For you to be healed, you have to let go and let God heal your brokenness.

At times I felt uneducated, especially when my aunt's children and others were going to school, and I was not. I used to stand by the gate and watch other children go to school while I did not. It hurts, but it helped me to accept that I did not have a solid educational background. Thank God He is not partial, and there was hope for me.

I would like to encourage those reading my book to trust God if you are going through rejection. I prayed and had a strong hope that my mother would return to take me away from my aunts who were so evil. God answered my prayer; He allowed my mother to obtain permanent status in Canada, so she could take me to live with her.

God can fix the wounds of a woman, the wounds of a single mother. Give them all to God. He will fix it for you and mend the broken pieces back together again. I believe that God chooses those who are broken and wounded to work for His kingdom. God wants to heal those wounds; He works through our pain and weaknesses. We have been battered, we have been bruised, we have been tossed about, but there is still hope. Do not lose faith in God; trust Him because there is hope.

Understand that these experiences have benefits. My experiences enabled me to encourage my sisters. You may not be able to see it now, but there are opportunities in your pain, so do not give up. Trust God for your change to come. "Trust in the Lord with all of your heart and lean not on your own understanding." (Proverbs 3:5 - NIV).

We do not always understand what happened or is happening to us, but God understands. God will never reject us; instead, He accepts, embraces, loves, and has confidence in us. Many people like to talk because it is easy to do so, but the experience that a person goes through is actually worth someone listening to. If I do not experience pain, struggles, or end up wounded, how can I tell you that there is hope? It is because of my experiences and what I have been through that enables me to tell you there is hope in God.

Experience provides something that nothing or no one else can give; We learn from real-life experiences. We learn in God's Word that experience makes a difference. People can listen to us because we have been through an experience. The world is filled with so many people who like to pass judgment when they are not aware of what you have been through.

I remember when I came to Canada in 1985, it was like my past was suppressed. I wanted to forget about my life in Jamaica so much that I suppressed it. It was not until I got married to my first husband and started to experience abuse and rejection that I recognized I was reliving my past. God sits on the throne and He sees and knows everything. There is hope. There is a song that I often sing: "I don't believe He brought me this far to leave me." When the pain got so hard, and I felt like my life was just turning upside down again: now a mother, abused wife, and all past abuse, I remembered that God said He would never leave or forsake me. God would never allow me to go through those experiences with the belief that nothing good was going to come out of it.

I do believe that God uses my experiences to help me to help others.

To the person reading this book, you may be going through a number of challenging experiences, but remember that there is hope. There is a reason God has allowed you to go through what you are currently experiencing. When we are hurting, we often tend to go through the motions and run to various individuals for help. However, believe that when you are feeling hurt and frustrated, and there is no one there to help, just talk to God. God is there with you, and He is allowing you to go through the situation because later on, you will be a blessing to someone going through that same problem you have been through. Jesus also suffered; He suffered on the cross. Hebrews 5:8-9 (KJV) states, "Though he were a Son, yet learned he obedience by the things which he suffered; And being made perfect, he became the author of eternal salvation unto all them that obey him."

Jesus needed the experience. He came down to earth in order to be our Priest, our mighty God. He came down to men so He could understand our pain and suffering. God wants to heal us; He wants to heal our body, mind, and spirit. God wants to take away all our wounds, so why not let them go and let Him take the wounds from us. Jesus came, and He suffered just like we are suffering. He had to come down because even He had to go through the experience. "...he was wounded for our transgressions, he was bruised for our iniquities: the chastisement of our peace was upon him; and with his stripes we are healed." (Isaiah 53:5 - KJV). Jesus suffered a lot, but in the end, He gained experience that enables us to look to Him. If Christ endured such pain and suffering, we can endure as well. I believe Jesus endured His suffering so He could equip us to help others in this world.

We should allow God to take the pain of our past and heal the broken pieces. He understands our weaknesses, frustration and pain because Jesus came and experienced suffering and pain. Therefore, God understands and wants to take those away from us. This is amazing! According to Hebrews 4:15, "For we have not an high priest which cannot be touched with the feeling of our infirmities; but was in all points tempted like as we are, yet without sin." (KJV).

We have been hurt and sometimes go through pain, but Jesus came down to this earth in the likeness of man, and He went through pain. Our God is good; He can take what Satan intended for harm and work it out for our good so we can help others. We are mighty soldiers in God's army. God wants to use us and take us from one level to the next. Therefore we need to let go of our wounds, give them to God and He will heal the broken hearted.

I can recall a time in my life when I was going through my divorce, and the brokenness, wounds, and scars of rejection were so bad that I attempted suicide three times. I was so broken, messed up, and felt rejected, but God was not ready for me to leave this world, so my life was spared. I was given another chance so I could come back.

If you are thinking about committing suicide because there are so many broken pieces in your life, know that God wants to make something beautiful out of your life. God wants to give you beauty for ashes, and He wants to mend the broken pieces. I want my story to highlight the fact that God will never leave you, and He will never forsake you. When the world, your husband, and even your family members turn their backs on you, know that God will never leave or forsake you. Trust and believe in Him; He will give you the desires of your heart.

God will give you a word as He did in Isaiah 41:10 (KJV): "Fear thou not; for I am with thee: be not dismayed; for I am thy God: I will strengthen thee; yea, I will help thee; yea, I will uphold thee with the right hand of my righteousness." God never makes a mistake;

He will make something beautiful out of you. He has molded me and taken me a long way. God has truly made something beautiful of my life. The challenges that you are experiencing will be made valuable through God. He is going to use your experience as a tool, a weapon that will allow you to help others.

I never thought that today I would be able to encourage someone, but just like in Isaiah 41, God gives hope no matter the pain you are going through. No matter how painful it may seem, things will get better; all you have to do is allow God to heal your wounds just like He healed mine.

As women, there are so many painful experiences that we go through. For me, as a little girl, I was scarred with the wounds of physical, emotional, and mental abuse; I was bullied, slapped, and rejected. In spite of the wounds, God was with me even at such a tender age. The battering continued in adulthood with social and extramarital abuse from my husband, who thought it was greener on the other side and walked out on me with three children. I had to take care of them all by myself until he was forced by the court to support them. The stress of life led to some serious wounds: betrayal from trusted friends, friends who lied on me, and so many other wounds.

A woman's life can become a subject of gossip. Those are wounds as well, but God can take them and give you beauty for ashes. God turned my wounds into a beautiful rose garden, and He will do the same for you once you allow Him to. God will fulfill His promise to you.

I have gone through some painful times in my life. I felt so imperfect; the wound of imperfection makes you feel as though you are not good enough, you are not pretty, and you have low self-esteem. These are wounds that are not from God but are rather brought on by other people: family members, spouses, friends, and people you trust. People you hold close will hurt you and scar your life forever. Well, they may have thought it was forever, but there is hope.

There is nothing in this world that God cannot fix; God can fix it for you; just give Him your worries and let go. I am a living testimony that broken pieces can be placed back together, and dead bones come alive. Give them all to God; there is no wound, no sore, and no brokenness that He cannot heal. Trust and believe that God will take away all the abuse: sexual, emotional, and otherwise.

The scars from the wound of sexual molestation is still there; the scar of my uncle-in-law attempting to rape me, but I could not speak of it because I would be beaten. My aunt would have flogged me and accused me of lying. So, I had to hold that physical level of mental abuse, which literally destroyed my mind.

Abuse as a child can be damaging; it is a violation of a child's rights. My encouragement to young girls, hurting women, and single mothers is: you do not have to stay in pain if you do not know who to talk to. You can talk to God; He hears and answers prayers and will mend your broken pieces. God hears, sees, and understands. Sometimes He allows us to go through certain circumstances so He can make something beautiful out of us, so we can help others. That is what I am doing right now. He mended my broken pieces so that I can help someone. If you are reading this book, know that God is with you. Do not give up hope. No matter what violation you have experienced, there is hope; give your wounds to God and let Him heal you. He wants to heal your spirit. He wants to heal you from the inside out.

If you do not know Jesus Christ as your Lord and Savior, now is the time for you to understand that He wants to take your wounds and broken life, and make something beautiful out of it. Give Him your wounds and let Him redeem you; let God complete you. It is guaranteed that God will take those broken wounds and put them back together. Things will get better once you give it all to God. John 10:10 explains that the devil only comes to steal, kill, and destroy the life of God's people. Do not allow the devil to steal your joy or the peace that God has given you. There is hope in God. Your pains, suffering, struggles; none of it will go to waste because God will turn it around for your good. You cannot have a testimony without the test. So, when you are going through, remember God is with you; He is with us. Give all your fears to God and let Him heal you; He healed me.

I have been through the valleys of the shadows of death, but I did not fear any evil because God was with me. Give God your broken pieces, and He will put you back together again. He will make something beautiful of your life.

Chapter 4

YOUR LIFE IS NOT A SECRET TO GOD

God knows your destiny. "Before I formed you in the womb I knew you, before you were born I set you apart; I appointed you as a prophet to the nations." (Jeremiah 1:5 - NIV). There is nothing in your life that you will, or have, experienced that God does not know about. He knows all about us; He knows when you are hurting, when you are happy, and when you are sad. There is no secret in your life that God does not know about.

We sometimes face many disappointments in our life, which we tend to keep to ourselves. We do this because we are afraid that the secrets in our lives will be revealed; we are afraid of someone finding out what we are going through, and we are afraid of the embarrassment. So, we tend to keep these things within us, not knowing that it is affecting us, our family, and our relationships. However, if we take our problems to the Lord, He is always there to guide and direct us. He is always there to take our pain and heal our wounds, if only we take them to Him and trust Him.

The only way we can fix our problems and our pain is by praying about them and sharing them with someone we trust. In order for us to be healed, we have to be willing to tell our story; we have to be willing to share our pain and our grief so others can know about the problems we face in life. This is sometimes the only way through which we can be healed. I realize that not many people are able to speak about their pain because of embarrassment or they may not have the Spirit to do so. It took me a very long time to even consider writing this book, but I realized that writing this book would bring about healing for both me and others who may be going through the same situation.

Soul of a Broken Woman

1 Peter 5:7 states, "Cast all your anxiety on him because he cares for you." (NIV). God knows our secrets; He knows all things about us, so we only need to give Him our pain and burdens. God cares about us, and He will help and heal us. The burdens are so hard to carry by yourself.

In the story of Peter, the fisherman, he was at sea, and the water was rough. He was not getting any fish; probably his net was a mess, all tangled up. It was not easy for him as he was out there fishing for a long time. However, the minute Peter cast his net into the water, he committed himself to a release from the struggles that he was facing. Like Peter, we need to do the same.

I am unloading my anxieties in this book: everything that is weighing me down, all my cares, and all the abuse that I have been through to God. All my inner secrets that God already knows, I am releasing them to Him because He cares for me. If you release your anxieties and pain to God, He will give you inner peace, just the same as He gave me.

I remember as a young girl growing up with my aunt in Jamaica, I would cry so many times because of the pain, rejection, emotional abuse, low self-esteem, and the feeling of worthlessness. I was so young that I did not tell anyone. I felt like I was dying inside. I was too young to understand, but little did I know that God knew my secret. He knew what I was going through, but, like I said earlier, He allowed me to go through certain experiences in life so I would be able to have a testimony today. I am sure that our heavenly Father is not blind or slack concerning His promises towards us. He pays much attention to us and what we are going through.

"Shall not God search this out? for he knoweth the secrets of the heart. Yea, for thy sake we are killed all the day long; we are counted as sheep for the slaughter" (Psalms 44:21-22 - KJV). There is no secret that God does not know. Therefore, when you are going through struggles, when you feel there is no hope for you, know that you can always talk to God. Trust God. He will never fail you; you can be sure that your secret is safe with Him.

We often look at our problems and anxieties and think that they are so big for us and cannot handle them. However, when we look to God, who already knows our secrets, we will realize and see how small and insignificant our problems actually are. God is merciful; He can accomplish the things that seem impossible to us. "...With men this is impossible; but with God all things are possible" (Matthew 19:26b - KJV).

I kept many secrets in my heart about my life experiences, but I realized that when I took my burdens to the Lord, I felt much lighter; I began to feel much happier. There is much freedom and peace in just knowing that God is with me. "Commit thy way unto to the LORD; trust also in him, and he shall bring it to pass." (Psalms 37:5 - KJV). Do not put limits on God. He will fix your brokenness and make you whole again. He is just waiting for you to come to Him. God says, "Come to me, all you who are weary and burdened, and I will give you rest." (Matthew 11:28 - NIV).

God has a plan and purpose for our lives. We are fearfully and wonderfully made in the likeness and image of God. He wants all of us to be free from pain and life experiences that are damaging. God wants to heal our hurt and brokenness.

Chapter 5

BREAKING FREE FROM THE PAIN OF YOUR PAST

When life hurts, when your heart feels pain, when you do not know what to do, when you feel like there is no hope, do not lose faith; God is standing by, and He will set you free.

For most of my life, I suffered a lot of pain: emotional, physical, mental, and spiritual. I suffered a lot of abuse throughout my life as a child and even into adulthood. I kept the pain so deep inside because I did not want people to know what I was going through. I suffered alone. You would see a smile on my face when you saw me, but you could not tell that there were emotional scars. I thought it was okay to keep these to myself but little did I know that these scars hurt me and made things worse.

The hurt and pain that I felt inside sometimes exploded. The explosion was not violent but it certainly would have created anxiety in the people that were closest to me. The pain would cause much unforgiveness, bitterness, and even hatred towards the people who hurt me. Despite all that I have been through, I can testify that I am free from bondage, free from pain, and free from the scars that held me hostage over the years. I want you to know that if you are going through pain and suffering, if you find yourself in bondage, there is hope in God. I know for certain that God never intended for any of His children to go through pain and suffering in such a manner. God wants the best for us.

Breaking free from bondage and pain is a process. In order for us to be free, we need to submit ourselves to God, and He will grant us the desires of our hearts. One of the greatest bondage that individuals often face in life is unforgiveness. I can speak of this because there was a time in my life when it was so difficult for me to forgive. I had so much bitterness towards my aunt, uncle-in-law, and ex-husbands. These people hurt me so badly, they treated me so wrong, but I learned to release them out of my heart and free myself from the bondage through forgiveness.

God wants us to forgive; that is one of His commands. God said that we should forgive those who trespass against us: "And forgive us our trespasses as we forgive those who trespass against us." (Mathew 6:12 – NIV). Forgiving someone who hurts you is one of the hardest things to do, yet it is one of the greatest things you could ever do to change your life. Jesus went on the cross with no sins of His own. He suffered, but just before He hung His head and died, His words were: "Father, forgive them, for they know not what they do." (Luke 23:34 - KJV). God expects us to do the same; we should forgive as the Lord has forgiven us. I know that sometimes the people we forgive do not deserve to be forgiven because of the pain they have caused us. They are not sorry for what they have done to us, but if we want to be like Christ, it is our responsibility to obey His command and forgive those who trespass against us.

When I think back over my life, and everything I have been through, I have come to realize that the only way to be free from my pain, bondage, and suffering is to forgive. If I walk around with anger and bitterness in my heart, I will never be healed.

God has helped me to find my way to freedom, and He will do the same for you once you allow Him to help you. God will fight for you. Remember, the battle is not yours, it belongs to the Lord; take all your burdens to Him and leave it there; He will make a way for you. Do not allow your past to dictate your future because God has a plan for you. Jeremiah 29:11 "For I know the thoughts that I think toward you, saith the Lord, thoughts of peace, and not of evil, to give you an expected end." No matter the challenges and circumstances that we sometimes face in life, never forget that God is with you and that His promises are true. He will never fail us.

When your heart hurts, remember there is hope. Look at yourself in the mirror and tell yourself that you are beautiful; you are fearfully and wonderfully made.

Think about the positive things around you. Though your heart may be shattered, those broken pieces can come together again.

Breaking free from your past and turning it into blissful freedom requires much self-affirmation. I often had to do a lot of self-talk; I had to talk to myself. I had to tell myself, "You cannot allow your past to dictate your future; you have to forgive yourself and forgive those who have hurt you." I had to stop harboring negative thoughts. Sometimes when I was alone, it was hard to stop thinking of past memories. Therefore, in order for me to release myself, I had to think positively. I had to release all those negative thoughts from my mind, and I had to learn to control my thoughts and what I allowed to linger in my mind. I had to think of myself as being worthy of God's best for my life.

Chapter 6
GREATNESS LIES WITHIN YOU

We all have greatness inside of us. We were born with an assurance of prosperity and hope; we are God's creation. He knew us before we were formed in our mother's womb (See Jeremiah 29:11).

In spite of all the challenges I faced over the years, I have always believed that there is hope. I was placed in a certain situation that seemed hopeless, but deep down inside, I knew there was hope. I believe in myself. I believed that one day I would become successful.

After finishing primary school in Jamaica, I was never given the opportunity to go to high school. I used to watch other children pass by going to school, but I never gave up hope. I felt deep within me that my day would come. It was not easy for me to watch other children doing some things that I would like to do, but I was determined to persevere amidst the odds. I was willing to work hard and ensure that I succeed in life. I was willing to produce the best of what was inside me, despite all the challenges and setbacks I had to face.

If you are faced with many challenges like I was, let me encourage and remind you that there is greatness in you. Finding that inner peace and greatness is a choice that you have to make; you have to tell yourself that you can do all things through Christ who gives you strength. You can tell yourself that you have worth and value.

You do not have to allow your past experiences to dictate your future. You have to know who and whose you are. You are in total control of what you become in life. If you allow your past experiences to dictate your future, then you have allowed yourself to lose control.

At one point in my life, when I felt I wanted to commit suicide, I had to take a self-inventory. I had to ask myself questions like, "Who am I? Why am I here? Is my life worth living?" Those were tough questions.

When life hits you so hard, the emotional pain will cause you to lose self-control. When this happens, I catch myself and reflect on my dreams. Tell yourself that you do not have to live in failure, but you can create something beautiful in your life. You do not have to listen to the lies around or other people's opinions of you. You do not have to listen to the negative things that people have to say about you because you know who you are, and you know what lies within you. Greatness lies within you: you have self-worth, you have value, and you are a success. I had to speak to myself: you have to speak life into yourself and break free from the bondage of disappointments, pain, and rejection. Break free from all the darkness that surrounds you; know who you are, and walk out of darkness into the light that lives within you.

Great happiness and success can only come from within. When you know yourself and know your worth, you allow your light to shine like a lighthouse on top of a hill that cannot be hidden. You have to take control of you; you have to take control of your life. You have greatness in you; you have life within you, and you have success within you. Believe in yourself, trust who you have become, and walk in your purpose. We should not have to live our lives at the mercy and expense of what happened to us. We have to allow ourselves to be in control of our lives.

In knowing who I am, I did not allow myself to be stuck in the prison of my past. I instead chose to leave the past behind so I could embrace the bright future in me with greatness, unstoppable confidence, and success. I knew what was within me; therefore, holding on to the darkness of my past would only sabotage my future; I was not about to let that happen. The greatness that is within me is to build a bright future. You can have that great confidence in knowing that your future is bright.

Soul of a Broken Woman

We were all fearfully and wonderfully made in the likeness and image of God. We were born unique for a reason. Stand out! We were born with greatness within us; we are unique in our own way and should be appreciated for who we are. Therefore, we should not dim the lights to fit into society or the background of other people's lives. We need to shine bright so that others will see our brightness and shine with us. There is nothing we cannot become if we believe in ourselves. I believe in myself; I believe that I can do anything I put my mind to, and so can you.

Trust the greatness you have within you; believe in yourself, believe in who you are. When you believe in yourself, you have great potential, and this potential becomes unlimited. This means that you can reach far beyond the skies, far beyond your imagination. All you have to do is believe in yourself and know that you are special.

I looked at the circumstances around me and the challenges I had to face, and decided to take it as a blessing instead of a curse. I believed everything and every experience in my life was exactly what it should be because it brought out the best in me. It allowed me to find myself; these experiences propelled me into greatness; they propelled me into finding my identity and purpose.

As a young girl growing up in Jamaica, there were so many uncertainties about the future. I could not and did not even know who I was because all I knew was verbal, emotional, physical, and mental abuse. It was almost as though I was accepting abuse because that was all I knew. Leaving that situation and arriving in Canada in 1985 to be with my mother, I started to see life in a different way. I had a different perspective of Life.

I went to high school shortly after my arrival in Canada. It was like a brand-new world as I started to see the light in me. I enjoyed school, and I did very well. I also got along with my high school teachers. I was now surrounded by people with positive influence that worked to propel me into my destiny.

Soul of a Broken Woman

I graduated from high school, went to college, and spent a few years there. I did very well as I graduated with honors from a few programs. I worked part-time during my college years, and upon graduating, I was able to obtain an awesome job within my field of study. All of this was not easy to accomplish; however, I learned how to let go of my fears and leap into the unknown.

Sometimes we allow the fears of our past to become obstacles in the path of our future. It is time to release the greatness that lies within you. We are so focused sometimes on what we cannot do instead of thinking about what we can do. What I have been through in life was not easy, but I learned to let go of my fears and take risks. I now know who I am. I have greatness within me; I have a great desire to succeed no matter what is going on around me.

When someone goes through life, and is being challenged by many adversities, it is not easy to see the greatness that lies within you. It takes courage and the ability to push through the pain, hurt, and disappointments. But one thing is for certain, I learned how to fight my way through. If you are faced with many challenges, adversities, disappointments, and setbacks in your life, do not be discouraged because there is hope for you. There is greatness within you; you just have to surround yourself with the right people who will help you find your destiny and people who will help you identify who you really are. You may be afraid, just like I was, but you have to face your fears and take risks like I did, and believe in yourself. You are a masterpiece created by God in His image and likeness.

God commanded Moses to take His people out of Egypt, but Moses had a speech impediment: he stuttered in his speech. Moses had challenges, so he did not think he was good enough or have the capabilities to do what the Lord was leading him to do. He complained that he could not speak well enough, and the Lord was asking him to lead the children of Israel out of Egypt. He thought he was not good enough to do it because he could not speak. God saw the greatness within Moses.

In the end, Moses was able to deliver the children of Israel out of Egypt.

We have good and bad moments in life. We are faced with challenges, some as early as from childhood, and we tend to focus on the bad. However, we should try to focus on the good. Although we are faced with these challenges in our lives, we should look at them as not all bad. If we keep focusing on the negative side of life, and how unfair life is or has been, we could end up missing the entire purpose of God in our circumstances. "And we know that in all things God works for the good of those who love him, who have been called according to his purpose." (Romans 8:28 - NIV).

Despite the unpleasant things that may have happened in our lives, we know that all things work together for the best, for those who love God. We have to believe with confidence, wisdom, and strength that we are overcomers, and we can do whatever we set our minds to do.

All the terrible things that I have experience in my

life reminded of Joseph in the Bible and all the terrible things that happened to him. I am reminded of how his brothers threw him in a pit, and he was sold as a slave. Joseph was lied on and accused of raping Potiphar's wife. He was thrown in prison, but Joseph had greatness within him. Therefore, whatever his brothers and other accusers meant for evil, God meant it for good. For that reason, Joseph became one of the greatest king; he had greatness within him.

I know we are faced with various circumstances; however, we can rely on God's promises. No matter what our circumstances are, no one can take the greatness of God from within us; we are unique. We have to believe in ourselves and believe that we can do all things through Christ who strengthens us.

Chapter 7

NEVER QUIT ON YOURSELF (BE THAT CONFIDENT WOMAN)

We are faced with many struggles and challenges in life. I have gone through years of many types of abuse and difficult circumstances. I had to face so many struggles and experiences, but I never quit on myself. This is why I am encouraging you through this book never to quit on yourself.

There were so many times when I wanted to quit. I wanted to give up on life, but I soon realized that quitting was not an option. I had to fight to survive. I had a reason to live. I knew if I quit, I would not be able to forgive myself.

In life, you will have failures; you will be disappointed, have bad experiences, many setbacks, and hang-ups, but never quit; never give up on yourself. Believe in yourself, knowing that every disappointment happens for a reason. You may not know why you are, or were, faced with certain circumstances, but despite the challenges, hold on to hope and never give up on yourself.

Speak life to yourself. Tell yourself you have to go through struggles in order to become successful. You have to go through something. Being the confident woman that you are, tell yourself you are valuable, tell yourself that you have worth, and you can make it despite many oppositions. I had to evaluate my life; I had to take an inventory of my life, and tell myself there is much for me to live for. There were people depending on me; I did not want to live with the talk of regrets. It is hard; I wish I did, or I wish I could. I want to make sure that I fulfill my purpose in life.

Never quit on yourself. There are many opportunities for one's success, so I encourage you to hold your head above the waters, and if you try the first time and fail, pick yourself up and try again because if at first you do not succeed, try and try again. Be persistent; the outcome of your trying may look uncertain, but be hopeful. If you fail to succeed in one opportunity, there are many other opportunities that await you. You must have determination and zeal to push through the struggles and the pain you face in life. When you are pressed down, you can rest if you must, but be encouraged, and do not give up. Even when life seems full of uncertainties, you can overcome your uncertainties and use them as life experiences. Regardless of the situation you are currently facing, the situation is not hopeless. Be persistent, and keep trying, even when life gets you down. You can't give up on yourself; not giving up on yourself could make a huge difference in others' lives.

I have learned from my experiences to never give up on myself. Not giving up on myself made all the difference in my life; this has helped me to change my perspective on life, and that was one of the reasons I wrote this book: to help you and others turn your lives around. I hope to serve as an inspiration for others to learn from my story and use my experiences to get through their own dark times. Staying true to your dreams could transform the world for the better, but this can only happen if you refuse to give up on yourself.

Do not allow your past to dictate your future. I have been through so many challenges, but no matter how many times I felt like giving up, I pressed my way through the pain. I stayed focused on my goals. My experiences and failures taught me valuable lessons that I used to propel me into my destiny. Quitting will never be an option for me.

Chapter 8

OVERCOMING

There are many people who faced adversity and serious setbacks in their lives but did not give up. I am one of those persons. I grew up in Jamaica without a father. I never knew my father, and at a tender age, my mother left for Canada to make a better life for me. It was never her intention to leave me at a young age, but she had to so we could have a better life. I lived with my aunt and experienced many forms of abuse. I did not get a chance to go through high school because I had to work like a slave. I suffered many scars and endured much pain, but I had faith enough to believe in myself in order for me to get to where I am today. I had to find the strength in me to build my self-esteem that was so badly deteriorated, wounded, battered, and bruised.

Challenges and adversities are difficult to overcome. It would not be a challenge if it was not tough. We all go through struggles and difficult times, but it is up to us to choose how we respond to them. In Jeff Olson's book, "The Slight Edge," he explained that: "There will be many obstacles placed in front of you during your lifetime. And you can determine the size of a person by the size of the problem that keeps them down."

I have learned that for me to overcome the many challenges that I faced in my life, I should never drown myself in self-pity and allow negativity to get the better of me. Instead, I learned to control the things I can and found the courage to deal with the things I cannot change. I have learned to surround myself with people who force me to do better, force me to see a brighter future, and people who encourage me to not dwell on my past. I often enjoy silence; this was where I found true wisdom and answers from God for some tough unanswered questions.

Soul of a Broken Woman

One of the most difficult things for me was letting go of my past hurts. I had the tendency to hold on to grudges, anger, and bitterness because of the things I have been through. The scars and pain I had to feel in my life helped me to realize that holding on to those things only kept draining me of true happiness. Therefore, I had to learn to let go of negativity. Holding on to challenges that we face will create a lasting impact on our lives. In order for me to move forward and overcome these challenges, I had to let go. It was not easy, but I had to let go for me to begin to see any change in my circumstances.

One of the ways I overcame my challenges was to focus on myself instead of the circumstances. I reminded myself that I could do all things through Christ who gives me strength. I also reminded myself that I could do anything I put my mind to despite all that I have been through. I believed in myself, and I told myself quite frequently: "You are beautiful, you are loved, you are special, and you are wonderfully and fearfully made in the likeness and image of God." We have to encourage ourselves sometimes. Eliminate self-doubt and embrace affirmations daily in order to be successful overcomers. "And David was greatly distressed; for the people speak of stoning him, because the soul of all the people was grieved, every man for his sons and for his daughters: but David encouraged himself in the LORD his God." (1 Samuel 30:6 - KJV).

Eckhart Tolle said, "This too shall pass." Whatever the obstacle or the challenge that is in your life at the moment, remember that this too shall pass.

Chapter 9

LIFE'S LESSON

Life is a process. I believe that my life has a divine purpose. All the struggles, hurt, and pain I had to go through all happened for a reason. I have learned to accept what happened to me and use the experiences to propel me into what I have become today. I had to encourage myself and use my experiences to create changes I knew would make me a better person.

My experiences helped me know that my circumstances were temporary and that my change would come in time, and I would have a happy and fulfilled life. Even though I did not understand why certain things happen in my life, I have learned to trust the process and trust God to take me to the next level.

One of the lessons I have learned was to stop focusing on the circumstances that surrounded me and look within myself to see if there was anything I could do to improve my circumstances. I understand that life is not fair and uncomfortable things happen to the best of us. Life's lessons have taught me, and will also teach you, how to make the necessary changes to propel you into your destiny. Everything happens for a reason: learn from them, encourage yourself, have faith and hope, and God will make that difference if we only believe.

There are some circumstances in life that we cannot control, but we can make choices. Therefore, we can either allow these challenges and circumstances to tear us apart and make us victims or we can rise above our circumstances.

I realized that I am in control of myself. Therefore, no matter what happens to me or what I have gone through: the hurts, pain, suffering, abuse, I am in control. I chose to bring myself into a safe zone by surrounding myself with good influences; people who encourage me to build on my self-esteem and continuous self-affirmations.

I have learned that I cannot change what happened to me in the past, but I have the power within me to ensure that those experiences are not repeated in the future. My attitude towards the things that I experienced certainly gave me a better attitude and perspective on life. Going through the challenges required much strength: mentally, spiritually, and intellectually. I had to stay strong and surround myself with people who had my best interest at heart, so I could get support to go through. I had to develop a positive outlook on life and understand that I may not be able to change the things that happened to me, but I had enough courage within to change the way I perceived life. So now I look at life in a positive way.

Oliver Wendell Holmes Jr. said: "A mind that is stretched by brand new experience never goes back to its old dimensions." There is a famous saying that when life hits you with a brick, you just really hate life. Having gone through all the struggles, I realized I was my worst enemy and had to do something about it. I had to forgive myself first, and then I had to forgive the people who hurt me. Forgiveness is the key to true happiness.

The most important thing that helped me and will help you overcome life's challenges is to focus on God instead of focusing on the problem surrounding you. "Fear not, for I am with you; Be not dismayed, for I am your God. I will strengthen you, Yes, I will help you, I will uphold you with my righteous right hand." (Isaiah 41:10 - NJKV).

Secondly, trust God's plan, even when it does not make sense. Remember, he knew you even before you were formed in your mother's womb (Ref: Jeremiah 29:11).

Thirdly, surround yourself with positive people who will propel you into your destiny in a positive way.

Soul of a Broken Woman

Surround yourself with people who can lift your spirit and remind you of all the positive things that are within you. This is how I was able to overcome some of my challenges. I had accountable and positive people who took the time and invested in my well-being.

"Challenges are what makes life interesting and overcoming them is what makes life meaningful."
- Joshua J Marine

"We don't develop courage by being happy every day. We develop it by surviving difficult times and challenging adversity."– Barbara De Angelis

YOU CAN FIND HEALING THROUGH SCRIPTURES

1 John 4:18 – NIV:

"There is no fear in love. But perfect love drives out fear, because fear has to do with punishment. The one who fears is not made perfect in love."

God's love is perfect. There is no fear in perfect love. God's love is unconditional.

Psalm 147:3 – NIV:

"He heals the brokenhearted and binds up their wounds."

God knows all about us. He knows our pain; He knows our sufferings, and He will heal your brokenness if you would allow Him.

Psalm 51:17b – NIV:

"A broken and contrite heart you, God, will not despise."

God is not ashamed of us. He loves us, and He will comfort us in our brokenness.

2 Corinthians 12:9 – NIV:

"But he said to me, 'My grace is sufficient for you, for my power is made perfect in weakness.' Therefore I will boast all the more gladly of my weaknesses, so that Christ's power may rest on me."

Matthew 11:28-30 – NASB:

"Come to me, all who labor and are heavy laden, and I will give you rest. Take my yoke upon you, and learn of me, for I am gently and lowly in heart, and you will find rest for your souls. For my yoke is easy, and my burden is light."

Isaiah 54:4 – NIV:

"Do not be afraid; you will not be put to shame. Do not fear disgrace; you will not be humiliated. You will forget the shame of your youth and remember no more the reproach of your widowhood."

HOW TO KEEP AND SUSTAIN YOUR HEALING

1. Invite Jesus into your suffering and struggles; He will comfort you.

2. Pray without ceasing.

3. Read your Bible and spiritual books regularly.

4. Commit yourself and ways to the Lord.

5. Do not be entangled again with the yoke of bondage; be free from Satan.

About the Author

Karen Brown is a severely, mentally, physically, and emotionally abused survivor. She was able to overcome all the struggles and obstacles she faced in her life. She is now thriving and living a fulfilled, God-fearing, and successful life, while pursuing her ultimate goal of one day becoming a family lawyer. She is a mother of three adult children, whom she single-handedly raised: a son and two daughters.

Hurts and sufferings are things that one can overcome. However, one must go through a process that does not happen overnight. Self-acknowledgement, counseling, and much prayer are needed to go through this process. For all the pain and suffering that she had gone through,

Karen believes that her purpose is to help women, particularly single, hurting women, overcome the many adversities they face in their lives. Karen hopes that her story will give encourage and bring hope to women who feel helpless and dismayed.

www.ingramcontent.com/pod-product-compliance
Lightning Source LLC
Chambersburg PA
CBHW071503070526
44578CB00001B/428